A Note to Parents

DK READERS is a compelling program for beginning readers, designed in conjunction with leading literacy experts, including Dr. Linda Gambrell, Professor of Education at Clemson University. Dr. Gambrell has served as President of the National Reading Conference and the College Reading Association, and has recently been elected to serve as President of the International Reading Association.

Beautiful illustrations and superb full-color photographs combine with engaging, easy-to-read stories to offer a fresh approach to each subject in the series.Each DK READER is guaranteed to capture a child's interest while developing his or her reading skills, general knowledge, and love of reading.

The five levels of DK READERS are aimed at different reading abilities, enabling you to choose the books that are exactly right for your child:

Pre-level 1: Learning to read
Level 1: Beginning to read
Level 2: Beginning to read alone
Level 3: Reading alone
Level 4: Proficient readers

The "normal" age at which a child begins to read can be anywhere from three to eight years old. Adult participation through the lower levels is very helpful for providing encouragement, discussing storylines, and sounding out unfamiliar words.

No matter which level you select, you can be sure that you are helping your child learn to read, then read to learn!

LONDON, NEW YORK, MUNICH,
MELBOURNE, AND DELHI

Produced by Southern Lights
Custom Publishing

For DK
Publisher Andrew Berkhut
Executive Editor Mary Atkinson
Art Director Tina Vaughan
Photographer Keith Harrelson

Reading Consultant
Linda Gambrell, Ph.D.

First American Edition, 2001
11 12 13 19 18 17 16 15 14
Published in the United States by DK Publishing
375 Hudson Street, New York, New York 10014
014-XA005-10/2001

Published in Great Britain by Dorling Kindersley Limited.

Library of Congress Cataloging-in-Publication Data
Hayward, Linda.
A day in the life of a police officer / by Linda Hayward. --
1st American ed.
p. cm.
ISBN-13: 978-0-7894-7954-9 (hb)
ISBN-13: 978-0-7894-7955-6 (pb)
1. Police--Juvenile literature. [1. Police.] I. Title.

HV7922 .H39 2001
363.2'3'02373--dc21   2001017393

Printed and bound in China by L. Rex Printing Co., Ltd.

The characters and events in this story are fictional and do not represent real persons or events.
The publisher would like to thank the following for their kind permission
to reproduce their photographs:
Key: t=top, b=bottom, l=left, r=right, c=center
DK Picture Library: 15; Dave King 27; Linda Whitwam 16t. **Models:** Donna Beck,
Scott Blake, Stacey Budge, James Evans III, Theresa Fox, Thomas Fox, Duke LaGrone,
Preston Nelson, Dillon O'Hare, John Springfield and Blitz, Jerry Suttles Jr., Kelvin Terry,
Vivian Terry, and Larry Wilhelm.

In addition, Dorling Kindersley would like to thank Sergeants Larry Wilhelm, Bob Copus and
the Homewood Police Department, Homewood, Alabama for props and location photography.

All other images © Dorling Kindersley
For more information see: www.dkimages.com

Discover more at
www.dk.com

DK READERS

BEGINNING
1
TO READ

A Day in the Life of a Police Officer

Written by Linda Hayward

DK Publishing

Joey is staying with his Aunt Ann and Uncle Bill.
Aunt Ann is a police officer.

After breakfast, Ann puts on
her badge and belt
and goes to work.

At lunchtime,
Joey and Uncle Bill
will meet Aunt Ann
at the police station.

badge

At the police station,
the sergeant talks
to the new shift.

sergeant

"Last night a bear escaped
from the zoo!" he says.
"Be on the lookout."

Ann and her partner, Jim,
are on patrol duty.
They pick up the keys
to their patrol car.

Ann and Jim patrol the west side.
Jim uses the two-way radio
to tell the station where they are.

two-way
radio

On Main Street,
Ann and Jim
look for signs of trouble.

At the corner of Main and State,
horns are honking!
The traffic light is broken.

traffic
light

Ann parks her patrol car.
She turns on the flashing lights.

flashing
lights

Jim calls the station.
"Broken traffic light
at Main and State," he says.
The station calls Traffic Repair.

Ann tells the drivers
when to stop and when to go.

At lunchtime, Ann and Jim
go back to the station.
Joey and Uncle Bill are there.

Ann gives them a tour.

"We have all kinds of
police officers," Ann says.
"Some of them ride horses!"

"Some police officers
ride bicycles," Ann adds.

"Some ride motorcycles...

and some work
with police dogs!"

police dog

"I like the police dogs best,"
says Joey.

Ann and Jim go back on duty.
They head down Elm Street.
Everything looks quiet.

Suddenly, Ann sees a boy crying.

Adam got off the bus
at the wrong stop!

Ann can help.
She shows him her badge so
he knows she is a police officer.

"Where do you live?" Ann asks.
Adam does not remember,
but he has it written down.
He opens his backpack
and shows Ann his ID tag.

NAME AND ADDRESS
Adam Mitchell
23 Willow Drive
Homewood
PHONE
135-2468

ID tag

Jim calls the station,

and the station
calls Adam's house.

Adam will be home
in five minutes!

Ann and Jim drive Adam home.
Adam's mother is very glad
to see him.

Oops!
Adam must give Ann
her hat back.

Back in the patrol car,
a call comes in from the station.
"Check out strange noises
at 203 Cedar Drive!"

Ann and Jim are on the way.

At 203 Cedar Drive,
the garage door is open.
The garbage can is tipped over.
What is going on?

Ann looks in the garage.
It is the bear that escaped
from the zoo!

Ann closes the garage door quickly.
"Call the zoo!" she shouts.

Two zoo keepers arrive
to pick up the bear.
Soon, everyone is safe,
and so is the bear.

Ann and Jim go back
to the station.
Their shift is over.
They turn in their keys
and write their police report.

police
report

When Ann gets home,
Uncle Bill has some news.
"A TV reporter called!" he says.
"She wants to do a story
about you catching the bear!"

Joey is excited.
"You're so brave,
Aunt Ann," he says.
"I can't wait to tell my friends."

Ann smiles.
She has the best job in the world!

Picture Word List

badge page 5

flashing lights page 11

sergeant page 6

police dog page 17

two-way radio page 8

ID tag page 21

traffic light page 10

police report page 29